24 SIMPLE AND EASY WAYS TO *GET RICH QUICK!*

Two Dozen Ways to Get the Wealth You've Always Wanted and Deserved.

By T.J. Rohleder
(A.K.A. America's "Blue Jeans Millionaire")
Founder of the Direct-Response Network

Also by T.J. Rohleder:

TABLE OF CONTENTS

INTRODUCTION:

Greetings! This is T. J. Rohleder with the Direct-Response Network of Goessel, Kansas, and I want to thank you very much for purchasing "24 Simple and Easy Ways to Get Rich Quick!" In this breakthrough publication, I'm going to share 24 proven strategies that can make you rich, *if* you're willing to put them into action and work hard. These strategies have made DRN and our parent company, M.O.R.E., Inc., truckloads of money and they've made lots of other people millions of dollars as well.

In kicking this off, I want to start out with why this is such an important product. The purpose of the Direct-Response Network is to help average people make *above*-average incomes. A lot of people are confused about making money and what they mean by "getting rich" can be very subjective. Some people think anyone who can afford to buy an extra bag of groceries a week is rich because those people can spend more money than they can. To others, rich means being able to buy anything you want whenever you want. It's all subjective, based on how much money you want to make and how much money you *need* to make.

In general, people need to acquire the "get rich" or the "be rich" mindset in order to be successful. Many of us who were brought up in moderate circumstances look at rich people as different than us because they're the folks who live in the special part of town, who drive the big cars, and have the big houses. It's kind of a "them and us" mentality. If you're in the middle-class somewhere, even if you're in the upper middle-class, you may have the mindset that you're just not one of these rich people and you weren't meant to *be* one of them. Well, you know what? Nothing could be further from the truth. Rich people, with the exception of the maybe 2-3% who inherit wealth, usually came from the middle-class anyway. They just found techniques and strategies that made them rich.

That's what I'm going to cover in this publication: I'm going to show you exactly what those other people did to make all their money. The principle behind this is very simple. If you can discover how other people got rich and then utilize the very same principles they used, then you can get rich, too. I'll even give you a head start — a push, if you will. I'll discuss what other people have done to get rich and provide some shortcuts using direct-response marketing strategies that can accelerate the process. Let's get started, shall we?

CHAPTER 1:

The First Five Secrets

The best place to start this publication is with a discussion of a university study that was once performed on two hundred self-made millionaires in an attempt to determine the common denominators they shared. Was there anything that these people were doing that the rest of the world wasn't? Was there some kind of formula these people had discovered that was uniquely similar in nature? Well, the study revealed lots of things. First of all, it was discovered that these self-made millionaires came from different backgrounds so heredity and class weren't in the picture. These people had different educational levels. Some were PhD's and some had never even made it through the 4th grade. However, the study found that almost all of them shared five characteristics and those are what we'll start our list of 24 success secrets with.

The first characteristic, **Secret Number One**, is that these people were all captivated by their work. Work is a four-letter word to about 90% of the people out there. That's often why they come to me and ask, "How can I learn some of the direct-response marketing techniques? I hate what I do. I hate the factory, I hate working for the government, or I hate being a health care professional." Well, If you hate what you do, then your chances of being successful are somewhere between slim and none. You know you have to spend time and exert effort to achieve results and, in the end, a lot of us end up hating what we do and feeling it's not worth the effort. This isn't the case for most self-made millionaires; work is something altogether different for them. If you're really passionate about or love what you do, as the old cliché goes, you never have to work hard in your life. You might work forty, fifty, sixty, even seventy hours a week sometimes and it might seem to others that you're working long and hard — but you're not, if you love what you do. No success can come to the man or woman who hates what he does or she does.

With these people, work's like a hobby. People get very much involved in every single aspect of their hobbies because a hobby is something that greatly interests them. It's something that excites them. Well, it's the same for people who love their jobs. They're working long and they're working hard. There's no question that some people, many people, in fact, have turned hobbies into millions. I once worked with a man who loves golfing; that's his hobby. He's perfected a gib, a heavy golf club that you practice your swing with. Then, when you actually get a real golf club in your hands, it's so light and so agile compared to this big, heavy metal type club that it's easy to handle. His gib has become a real success in the golfing magazines so he's making money at the thing that he loves best.

You should ask yourself, "What am I best at? What do I love the most?" Years ago, when we did our Blue Jeans Millionaire seminars, we tried to teach people that everyone has something about them that's unique and special and it was up to them to find out what that is. Then they need to understand that around the world there are tens of thousands, perhaps even *millions,* of people who share those very same interests. With the specialty publications, the Internet, and the online newsgroups, you can reach people of all topics and interests.

This reminds me of something Russ von Hoelscher, my

friend and mentor, once told me about. About 30 years ago, he did some business with two brothers in Duluth, Minnesota. Their favorite thing in the world, other than their families, was fishing. They ended up designing, creating, and eventually manufacturing a whole line of fishing lures. They made a ton of money and eventually sold the company to a major fishing tackle company. That's another example of hands-on work by a couple of people who became wealthy doing the things they loved best. Every day wasn't work, then.

Some of the people who know my wife Eileen and I think we're workaholics and they think our lives are somehow shallow because of it. The thing about our lives is that the whole business of mail order has been so exciting to us. It's basically like a hobby is for most people. It's not all that unusual for us to still be up at 10:30 talking about business and all the ways to develop new products and new ideas for making money. We never had that at regular day jobs. A job is something that you just go to, at the end of the day you have this little card that you punch into a machine, and then you collect your check at the end of the week. That's all it is.

If you learn some of these techniques and you currently have a job, whether it's a white-collar or blue-collar job, you ought to be very aware of what's going on around you. The various tools, implements, or things that you use in your work could all be things that need improvement. Whether you work in an office, factory, or retail store, you can often find things in your job that you can make better. You can print or publish something in the form of a booklet or book that would help people that are doing this type of work. So, often you can turn a boring job into a successful business of your own, if you just find ways to improve the type of work you do. Or, you can do things on the side. You can start a sideline with direct-response marketing or a similar type of business; you may need your job for security purposes, but in the off hours you could be doing what you love to do. Eventually, that could turn into a full time enterprise.

That's exactly how Russ von Hoelscher started out about 35 years ago. He was working at a state mental hospital as a recreational therapist and, although he rather liked some aspects of the job, the pay was terrible. There was a lot of depression there because of the mental illness, too, with so many mental and alcoholic patients. That's when he started his mail-order business on the side and it built up for a year and a half before he quit the hospital. That's a powerful technique that can work just as well today, if not better, because of recent elaboration of computer technology. It's so much easier now. The computer has made it simple to isolate and find people of like minds. There are so many ways that we can link up with people of similar interests that it's much easier than it was when Russ or I started out. The more technology grows, the better off we're going to be, as far as being able to target the people we want to get in contact with.

The second quality that the study found, our **Secret Number Two**, is *persistence*. This has been a big quality that my wife Eileen brings to our partnership and it's contributed a great deal to our success. When she gets her mind set on doing something, there's nothing that can budge her. That's also a principle those professors found for all the successful entrepreneurs in their study. Persistence really separates the winners and the losers — as the old cliché has it, "Quitters never win, and winners never quit." That may be a cliché, but only because it's a basic truth. The people who are persistent, who don't give up when the going gets rough, are the ones who make it. You can knock them down a dozen times and they'll get up thirteen times. Knock them down twenty times and they'll get up twenty-one. They realize that you can have a string of failures and still win in the end. They've learned this the hard way and still continue to go forward.

Why? Because once you start to achieve some success, one major success can wipe out all the previous failures. Many people give up after just one or two tries and, often, the tries are half-hearted to begin with. Some people just give up way too soon. They don't realize that the longer you stick with something, the easier it gets — and the more you increase your odds of hitting it big. I very seldom meet a man or a woman who is persistent and determined to make it in business who doesn't. Sure, I've seen some who have success come early and others who've had to struggle for a while. But most of the real failures I've seen have been those who have tried one or two things that probably weren't the best type to start with in the first place. They were unsuccessful. They lost some money and then they go around telling everybody else, "Mail-order doesn't work. Multi-level marketing doesn't work. Direct response marketing doesn't work." And you know what? That's absolute bull!

Just as an example, Eileen and I had to try lots of different things before we made it. We had many, many failures along the way. We started out with a lot of dreams; we were dirt poor and we wanted all of the nice things in life. We tried dozens of different multi-level marketing companies. We tried dozens of other ways to make money, too, and everything failed until we found the direct-response marketing business. I give Eileen all the credit for that because I was always one of those quitters. I was one of those people who bailed out as fast as I could at the first sign of anything going wrong. It was because of Eileen's quality of being able to stick with things that finally we were able to turn that around. God bless her for that.

Winston Churchill was once asked to give a speech to a group of college graduates. They wanted him to share all of his wisdom and say something that could really inspire these kids. He got up to the podium and there were hundreds of students just sitting there, ready to listen to every word he had to say. The whole place went quiet. He got up and said, "Never, never, *never* quit." Then he went right back and sat down where he was sitting before. That was his entire speech, just those four words — and that was the most inspiring thing that he could possibly say. They asked him afterwards, "What made you think of this? We've never heard such a short message with such a powerful theme." He said, "World War II was raging and the Nazis were bombing the hell out of London and other British cities. That was on my mind as I was dealing with Nazi Germany and World War II. It's a message for myself; and then, of course, it would help the students in their lives."

The third thing that the study found — **Secret Number Three** — is that all those people who made millions and millions of dollars basically started from scratch. They were all super-competitive in the game of business. Making money is a lot like a game, you see. Some of the richest people I've ever met say money's important, but many of them have always said to me, "You can only eat so much steak or lobster. The house you have is nice, and sure, you could have a second vacation house — but you can only drive one car at a time." The point is, you reach a point where money isn't as important to you as it once was. What's important, at that point, is using money to keep score in the game, what you can do with that money, and how you can use that money to help other people grow. Look at all the wonderful things Bill Gates has done. He's become a multi-billionaire, but he's also created hundreds of other millionaires within his company. So when you get rich, your prosperity goes through the roof. You can take a lot of people with you and that's a beautiful thing. Competitiveness is what's needed. You feel you're as good as anybody else and you're willing to play the game to its fullest. You want to win and you keep score by the money.

It's important to keep an eye on the competition and figure out how you can beat them, but the main person you should compete with is yourself. I think that's very important, as long as you're always willing to find ways to give people better service than the competition. How far can you go? Well, in this study of two hundred self-made millionaires, they found that those people were all very competitive, and were willing to do whatever it took. That's the fourth quality the authors of that study found, our **Secret Number Four**: they had that mental attitude that made them do whatever they needed to (within limits, of course) to succeed in business. This is related to the quality of persistence, but it goes beyond that because it means you'll take the next step as you go forward. You'll do whatever it takes. You won't make a bunch of excuses. You won't blame others for your failures. People will often blame their boss for being a jerk, say the economy was bad, claim that everybody was against them, that they were too young or too old, or that they didn't have enough education. That's all bunk.

Most of the time, success is lost only when we won't persist, when we don't set our goals, and we won't do what it takes to succeed. It's so important that you're willing to do whatever it takes to make some sacrifices and to turn off the boob-tube. People watch TV for too many hours a day. So, what if you watched two hours less television a day and applied it to your business? You'd say, "Well gee, I like *Big Brother* and *Survivor*, but what is that going to do for me in my old age?" What's going to be good about that when you're seventy or seventy-five? Take action for yourself. Be willing to do what it takes and do things for yourself that will bring you success.

Everybody says they want to make more money, with the possible exceptions of certain religious groups that think poverty is a virtue. If you get a poll of a hundred people and ask, "Would you like to make more money?" almost everyone will say "Yes!" Of course they want to make more money — but what are people willing to do? I don't want to mention anyone specifically, but we all know people who want nice things in life. When they drive by those big houses, they're like I used to be: very envious of rich people. I wanted all those nice things, but what I failed to realize at the time was that the people that lived in those houses paid a heck of a price to get what they got in life. What are you willing to give up to get to that point? Only a foolish person would ever expect great and wonderful things to come to them without putting in the necessary work.

Not to knock TV so much, but I'm just amazed at how many people spend their whole life at a dead end job they hate, then they come home and watch five or six hours of TV after supper, and then when asked to come to a seminar or contact me by mail or phone, they say, "Aww, I don't have the time to start a part-time business." The truth is that they *do* have the time, but they're not willing to give up a few simple pleasures *that really won't help them much in the long run.* One or two hours a day is all it takes to start a part-time business — but the chances for success are very, very slim for someone who won't even do that much. And it's not just TV. Some of these people I'm talking about play baseball five nights a week. They've got one night free and maybe they go out to dinner and to a movie. Well then, let's cut the back on baseball a little bit. Does that earn you any money? Heck no!

Sure, all of us only have so much time every day. I know that some people think that Eileen and I live very shallow lives because we don't socialize with a whole bunch of people. We don't have a constant blur of activities outside of our business that demand our time and attention. We live focused lives. Again, we're doing what we love to do and it's fun for us to be involved in the businesses we're involved in. At the same time, we're not out there wasting our energy on other things. You have to be focused and then you have to find something that you really want to do. This gets back to the desire and the passion. You'll turn off that TV or you'll not go bowling as much. You'll turn down going to a movie only if you can see beyond the dark horizon to the light of success, if the work you're doing is work that you enjoy.

Eileen and I do watch a little television every night, but many times we have a paper pad right next to us on the armchair on which we sketch out ideas. We've actually written lots of classified ads while we're watching a football game on a Sunday afternoon. Even then, we're still focused on the business. Our friend Russ von Hoelscher does the same thing. He's kind of a sports nut who watches a lot of football and basketball. But when he's watching, he has a yellow pad and pen in his hand and he's taking notes. Often he'll get lost in writing ads, writing copy, or jotting down ideas for the next week. Then all of a sudden, he'll hear some accelerated noise. He'll look up and someone scored a touchdown, but no problem, with instant replay they show it again. He watches it and gets into the game a little bit, then he fall back into his notes. He finds this is a good way to watch television and still do something productive.

The fifth and last common denominator that I'll talk about in this chapter, **Secret Number Five**, is the fact that all these self-made millionaires are goal-directed. What's the easy way to use goals in your life? Well, I'd say you've got to set your goals on paper. I've heard that from everyone: Dennis Waitly, Zig Ziegler, Jim Rowan, Anthony Robbins, on and on. You have to put down on paper, *not* just in your memory bank, exactly what you want to do. *You have to set goals.* Most people have heard it; they know about it; but nevertheless, they don't *do* it.

I've always had lots of problems with goals because, for one thing, goals take self-discipline — which is to say, you have to be somewhat disciplined if you want to get rich. I've always had a problem with that and it wasn't until I started writing goals down that I started experiencing real success. One of the things that the famous motivational speaker Jim Rowan says, in regards to goals, is that it's not so much what you accomplish as the journey that's important. It's who and what you become in the progress of working towards these goals. Another popular cliché I love is this: "Success is a journey, not a destination." We'll never ever reach our ultimate success because someday we're going to die. So while we're on this journey of success, we have to enjoy the journey. Even going on vacation, as everyone has done numerous times, I've noticed that the destination often doesn't often live up to the expectations. The journey, the drive, the airplane ride, or the boat ride, should be fun. You have to enjoy the journey because it's just as important as the destination.

CHAPTER 2:

Secrets Six Through Ten

Now that we've covered those five major areas that were emphasized in the study of 200 self-made millionaires, I'll move on to talk about some of the principles I've learned myself. Before I start that, though, I want to say something more about goals. The fact of the matter is, I really have no set goals. I realize that anytime an opportunity shows itself to me, I grab a hold of that opportunity and I usually buy into it. A lot of times, the opportunity that shows itself to me is bigger and better than any kind of goal I could have set for myself.

I think, sometimes, that goals are just directions — and that sometimes people are afraid to set goals because they're afraid of writing something in stone. Well, it doesn't have to be quite so hard and fast. Often, a good goal is a target that you're aiming for. As I mentioned in the last chapter, it's a journey, not a destination. I've noticed that in business, plans can change very often. Bigger and better opportunities come along, so the original goals you set are modified. I still think it's probably a good idea to have the goal direction, but you need to be very flexible and willing to look at other opportunities to make changes. So don't be afraid to change things as you go because you really learn things that way. I know that some of the most valuable techniques, methods, and strategies that Eileen and I have learned to get rich came as a direct result of actually getting in there and working on lots of things at once.

Tony Robbins has said that people will do more to avoid

pain than to gain pleasure. I think that's true. When we first started this business, we were so broke that we couldn't even pay the electric bill some months. Our only goal when we first started was just to make more money and never be there again. One most important goal was being able to survive during the wintertime. When we had a carpet cleaning business, nobody ever called us in the wintertime to come clean their carpets. That's why we got into the mail-order business and ended up making millions of dollars. We really didn't get in it to get rich. We got in it to *survive*. Once we got in it to survive, all these opportunities showed themselves to us. We just kept going with the flow, grabbing ahold of these opportunities as they came up.

One of the things that we had going for us was **Secret Number Six** on our list: a strong desire to get rich. Although Eileen and I started out just wanting to survive, we did have that strong desire to have all the nice things in life. Napoleon Hill and many others have talked about this in great detail. One book that you should definitely read is *Think and Grow Rich*. Now, you might say, "Oh, I already read that book several years ago." Well, you read it again! I've read it five or six times at least, and I find each new reading gives me new insights. In my opinion, Napoleon Hill is the greatest get rich coach you can have. One thing he pointed out was that the level of your desire to get rich will often determine whether you achieve your desire. As Joe Carbo once said, "Most people are too busy earning a living to make any real money." He was right about that because we get so tied into the daily chores of life just to keep the family together, or to keep our business together, or our job, that we forget to go beyond that. We have to have the big desire and we have to be able to think about what we need to do, to achieve big goals to get rich.

Eileen and I started this business with the goal of just being able to survive during the winter, but we wanted more than just a job. Even though we tried so many different ways to make money and we failed at so many different things, we still had that very powerful desire to have the nice things in life that many of our carpet cleaning customers had. We used to go into these huge houses owned by doctors, lawyers, and dentists and we used to wonder why we couldn't have all of those nice things, too.

One of our biggest goals is to help our employees at M.O.R.E., Inc., and all the distributors and other people on the sidelines, to succeed. That's one goal that drives us the hardest. It's not just the money, and that brings me to **Secret Number Seven** right there: you have to have a lot of reasons to get rich. One of the things I mentioned earlier is that money can only buy so many things; you've got to have more reasons for success than the money alone. Our mentor, Russ von Hoelscher, has told me that, when he started out, he was just thinking about the money and what it would buy. He wanted a new Cadillac and he got that. Then he wanted a home on the lake when he was living in St. Paul, Minnesota, and he got that. Then pretty soon it dawned on him, he said, that it's just like that song: "Is This All There Is?" You know, a Cadillac or a Mercedes is great; a new home is nice. It's good to be able to travel where and when you want. But you reach a point, sooner or later, where you look at yourself in the mirror in the morning and you say, "Is this all there is?" That's why I think you have to have a lot of good reasons why you want to be rich. In my opinion, they have to include things you can do with the money that'll help others. We don't just say this because we're nice people — hopefully we are! — but because it's a genuine get rich principle. Use some of your money to help other people in their businesses, to help your employees, and also to make donations to worthy causes. It seems to me that as you start to bless other people, you're also blessed. Whatever goes around comes around.

In many ways, that's even easier than setting goals or trying to come up with all of the reasons why you need to make so much money. Nowadays, our main focus is on trying to help everyone. That's where we put all of our emphasis. We really want to help people make money and we make that our primary goal — and it helps us in the end. Sure, we get some satisfaction out of the material things — we're human, after all! But the material things along don't produce the real feelings of satisfaction and fulfillment that you get inside. You need things *beyond* the physical. Focusing on the physical world will leave you empty. Now, I know a lot of people out there who've never experienced a lot of money; they may not really get what I'm saying. They say, "Just give me the money; I've been poor too long." I understand that, but when you do get the money, you'll see that there has to be something else in life because even money can leave you with an empty feeling if you don't have a purpose.

Like the proverb says, "Give a man a fish, and you feed him for a day; teach a man to fish, and you feed him for a lifetime." That's what I'm trying to do right here: figuratively teach you to fish. I want to teach you how to make your own money instead of handing people cash. I think that's the trouble with our welfare situation today: we've thrown money at the problem instead of teaching people how to make and handle money. We have to reeducate people so that they can get off their duffs, make money, and improve their own lives. Throwing money at the problem has proven to be worthless.

One of the ways that people can get started making all this happen for themselves is our **Secret Number Eight**. You have to think BIG. So many people used to have a dream when they were younger: they wanted all of the nice things in life, but then they got too busy earning a living to see to it. They lost their dream of doing big things and settled for a job of some kind. Don't let yourself fall into that trap: learn to think BIG. When you start your business, you might start with only a few hundred dollars; you might start with just a few classified ads to generate business. But remember this powerful principle that has helped me so many times: if you can learn to make a small profit of $50 or $100 in a magazine or a newspaper ad using direct-response marketing techniques, then you increase it — and not just a little bit. You can just keep adding the zeros if you work at it.

One of the greatest success principles for direct-response marketing is: Learn how to make a profit, even if it's a tiny profit. Once you've done that, increase your level of marketing. Go to more publications. There are so many newspapers, magazines, on-line services, radio, and television out there that you can use to turn a small profit into millions of dollars, simply through the law of increase. Most people just think too small. Whenever they come up with a money-making idea, they don't think about all of the ways they can expand it. Eileen and I have discovered that nearly every idea people have about making more money is either one of two things: they're either thinking way too small or they think about creating some mass merchandise marketing idea and getting some factory to pay them huge royalties. This is impractical for most people.

Let me share a story of a person that I know in Santa Barbara, California, who started out with a couple of little ads for some opportunity booklets that he placed in various newspapers. He started with a couple hundred dollars. He found about ten newspapers where the booklets were selling well and he got his hands on all the money he could — he borrowed from relatives and friends and increased his reach to a hundred newspapers, then two hundred, then five hundred, and then a thousand. That gentleman eventually built himself a business that averaged half a million dollars a week. He found a couple of little ads that worked in a couple of newspapers and, a year later, he was in a thousand newspapers taking in $2,000,000 a month. He thought bigger than most people did; he reasoned that if it would work in this little paper and that little paper, then it should work in the thousands of other papers in the country. He was right.

That brings me to another point, **Secret Number Nine**. When you study the lives of rich and successful people, you'll find that they're almost always in some type of business for themselves. No one will ever get rich by working for someone else — with a very a few exceptions, of course. For example, Bill Gates has a couple of hundred millionaires on his payroll that he's helped become rich. But that's very, very unlikely because it only happens to a tiny percentage of people. Ninety-nine percent of the time, you've got to control your destiny if you're going to be rich. That means a business of your own. For the most part, God helps those that help themselves and the best way to help yourself is to get in business for yourself.

Then you have to learn something about marketing and selling. I realize that's not everything, of course, because it definitely takes some talents in terms of organization, managing, and all the things you have to do to run the business. My wife, Eileen, was the one who brought those things to our team. But none of those things can happen unless you first learn how to bring the money in. A lot of the people who come to our seminars have questions about what it takes to be in business for themselves — but all they think and ask about are things like, "What kind of form do I need to take to this government office?" "What type of insurance papers do I need to fill out for this?" All that should be secondary to all the different ways they could bring the money in.

Sometimes, at these seminars, we're talking about how to publish books, manuals and reports, and make money as a self-publisher or information marketer. Often, we spend a lot of time answering questions like, "How do I copyright this?" Well, self-publishing information products is a relatively simple process, and there's no question that it's a good idea — but I'm amazed at how many people don't think about what type of informational product to acquire, how to produce it, or how to market it. Instead, they agonize about the nuts and bolts of the legalities. I think that that's a big mistake. You can get someone to take care of that for you at a very reasonable fee. What *you* have to do is get or create a good product, then learn how to market the hell out of it. Four or five months after we started our business, I'd had enough of the bookkeeping mess, so I just took it to an accountant and said, "Here, you take over." When you get that money coming in, you know for sure that that product is going to sell, and everything is going to fall together like you

23

want it, there's no need to do all the business stuff yourself.

We had a guy that came to one of our seminars and I'll never forget him (though I certainly wouldn't mention his name). This man had dreamed of starting his own business for probably twenty years. He had a great job, paying about $80,000 a year — what we call the "golden handcuffs." He had so many benefits it wasn't even funny, but for twenty years he had saved up all of his money that he could. He had a regular investment program because he dreamed of going into business for himself. He thought BIG! He did just what we said. He knew that if he wanted to get rich, he had to be in business for himself, and he was dreaming about making millions. So he spent $150,000 in cash building this huge, elaborate office set-up, with all kinds of phone lines, a president to run his company, and a comptroller to keep track of everything. He spent $150,000 before he brought in one single dime — and he didn't even know what kind of product to sell.

Now, you have to think big, but you have to also be practical, too. Don't put the cart before the horse. First, find something that will generate the capital. *Then* get the office if you need one — and you may not. I know people making a million dollars a year that work at home. But if you want the office and all the other trappings, you can have it. Just get the vehicle that's going to make you the money *before* you spend money on all these secondary things that aren't that important in the beginning. Otherwise, you're paying people with money that should be going into your pocket or back into advertising. It's ridiculous that so many people think of the *trappings* of business instead of thinking of the core things — which are the product and the marketing — things that can bring them the customer and make the business take off.

Secret Number Ten to getting rich is to use leverage. Everybody's always talking about the rich people who have so much time to spend out on the golf course or just goofing around all day. A lot of that is due to the fact that these people are using leverage. They don't have any more hours in the day than we do. They have to work through other people, just as they have to work through other situations that help them make money. That's the beautiful thing about direct-response marketing. It's often remote control selling. If you open up a little store, you're somewhat limited to the people in your neighborhood or the immediate area. When you're doing business by direct-response, you can do business all over the United States of America, Canada, and the world. J. Paul Getty, America's first billionaire, once said, "Give me 1% of the efforts of one hundred people rather than just 100% of my own effort." He believed in utilizing people and marketing techniques that would give him leverage. Even if you have a business that is basically local, you still can use leverage.

Russ von Hoelscher once owned a motion picture theater in St. Paul, Minnesota, years ago. He found that the previous owners charged about two dollars a seat from 11:00 A.M. to 10:00 P.M, the hours they were open. Russ let the theater stay open twenty hours a day and reduced the price to one dollar. Instead of having thirty or forty people taking up those 335 seats, he tripled the amount of people that would come to the theater. Lowering the price, putting ads in various coupon books, and employing other ways to encourage people to come to the theater was using leverage. Now, with any retail business, even one like Russ's, you're somewhat limited to the locals. That's why I love direct-response marketing: you can market all over the world. You can take one ad that's successful in one magazine and eventually put it in one hundred magazines. You can take a direct mail promotion that you mailed out 5,000 copies of with a good result, and you can make arrangements to increase that to perhaps a 100,000 mailings a month. You can quadruple or sometimes make a hundred times the profit from the same level of effort.

One night, we received a phone call at our house. One of our distributors wanted to know about a copywriter that we've used. He told me that his business was so tiring because he was doing all the bookkeeping, the copywriting, and everything else himself. I said that what he needed was to get some leverage: to hire an accountant to take care of that stuff. You decide what you're good at and do only that. I think that this is such a powerful idea that you can use it right this very minute. Find what you're the best at and *do* that. Delegate the rest to outside vendors. Remember, with direct-response marketing, and also with MLM, leverage is important because you can get distributors. In the Direct-Response Network, for example, we're making available various distributorships and we're giving our distributors the absolute power to make a lot of money. We're not shortchanging them; we're giving them far more than other people do in such distributorships, in fact. We're willing to take a small profit from many good distributors rather than to try to make it all ourselves. That's the key principle of MLM, of course: you get others to duplicate what you're doing. It's the secret of success if it's done right.

CHAPTER 3:

Secrets Eleven Through Fifteen

So far, I've shared ten great secrets of success. **Secret Number Eleven** is simply this: If you want to be successful, you have to look for other successful people to model yourself after. I think it's absolutely essential that you do this, just as it's essential to do the corollary and stay away from negative people. Now, if one of those negative people happens to be a spouse, parent, or a very close friend, you do have a problem. For family reasons, you have to listen to what they say, but not incorporate it completely. Negative people (some of who are very well-meaning) will drag you down. Just think about the four or five most successful people you know or admire and then think about why you admire them. What do these people have that you want? Make a list of the qualities, virtues, and power that these people seem to exude. Think about these people and about how to use their strongest attributes in your own life.

I also think you need a mentor — at least one — and hopefully more. Russ von Hoelscher has functioned as our mentor for years, starting from the times we'd hire him to come over for a $2,500 weekend right up until today — and it's been a profitable experience for both sides, I think. E. Joseph Cossman, who wrote the book *How I Made a Million in Mail Order*, was Russ's mentor right after he read the book. Russ just decided to follow his key techniques and his strategies as best as he could; and as soon as he found out where he lived and what his phone number was, Russ called him up. Joe graciously talked to Russ, who bought some more materials and newsletters from him. Then, eventually, Russ arranged with another guy to have him come and speak at a seminar and Russ took off from there. So, find yourself a mentor. Be willing to spend some money with that mentor, because what you can learn from a good mentor can be worth a hundred times more than every dollar you give to them. We need role models, and we need mentors so that we follow proven footsteps that lead to success.

I often feel, as I mentioned in a previous chapter, that a lot of people believe that the rich or successful people in this world have something that the rest of us don't have. That's not so, and it's obvious to anyone who will look closely. In fact, if they did study the lives of these successful people, they'd find out that these people are, in many cases, just following the lead of others. There's a certain pattern, a certain formula, or a certain set of actions that these people are taking; so if you want what they have, all you have to do is the same thing that they do. Model what they're doing. Success is predictable and success can be duplicated. There are certain things successful people do that unsuccessful people don't or won't do, so follow the successful, not the unsuccessful. Never envy the rich! Join them instead. Realize that you're just as good as anybody and can do anything that anyone else is doing. *Rich people are no different than we are*. I know this because I've been around too many of them. They have the same hopes, dreams, fears, and worries that you do. Sure, they have great characteristics, but they also have some characteristics that aren't so great. They're just people. They've found techniques that work in business that can make them a lot of money. If you follow and model what they're doing you can have the same success. Don't envy the rich:

become one of the rich.

It all starts with your mind and with the way you think about things, which brings us to **Secret Number Twelve** in our continuing series. That is: you have to sell people what they want, not what they need. This is a mistake a lot of people make. For example: in a seminar a few years back, we had one lady call in from Virginia who told us she'd put together a bulletin board for people to call in to do a survey. She wasn't getting many calls. I kept trying to tell her that her problem was that she was trying to get people to call in for a certain subject that *she* wanted to get information on, not something *they* wanted to get involved in. That's crucial: you've got to give people a subject they want to get involved in — for example, the top things in the news now, not something that you're really involved in yourself. Give the people what they want. Most people who fail at business make the mistake of trying to sell people what they *need* — or think they need — instead of what they *want*. People also make the mistake of trying to sell people what they *want* to sell them and that usually ends in defeat. You have to sell the public on the things they want, not the thing you want to sell them.

Every product or service has something within it that people want, but some products are a lot hotter than others. If you want to make the most money, you try to find those products that are the "hot spot." I once talked about marketing to a man who owns a small manufacturing company, who struggled for years to get this thing off the ground. I was giving him some ideas that he could use to sell his product by specifically going after a targeted market and showing how his product could solve the wants and desires that that market had. He told me that when he first got started, he didn't know very much about marketing, selling, or anything. He wrote a brochure for his product; he sent 400 of them out and he was so in love with his product that he really expected all 400 people to order his product. He was shocked when he didn't get one single order. Not one. This goes to show that sometimes you may love your product, but you don't stop to realize that other people aren't going to be in love with it like you are.

In order to really succeed, you have to hit the points that are beneficial to the reader; you have to tell them exactly how your product benefits them. You should always keep in mind that the key motivators for marketing are health, wealth, and happiness. Wealth, of course, can be related to greed or making more money. Health has a lot to do with longevity and living a more productive, rewarding life. Happiness, of course, is more of a state of mind, but it relates to pleasure; it can also relate to love or sex. Keep these things in mind because the great offers incorporate one or more of them: health, wealth, or happiness. There's no question that these are the major motivators or some adjunct to them; in other words, they're the broad topic. You can plug in many, many motivators under them. The idea is to show people how they can achieve those things with your type of product. Also, remember the flip side of wealth, health, and happiness. For example, with wealth, the flip side is that you can sell people products that will prevent them from losing money. The flip side of health is that people want to avoid discomfort and pain. With happiness, the flip side is that people want to avoid unpleasant circumstances and situations. So, in this sense, marketing is always a two-sided coin.

Often, when inexperienced people think about ways to make money — that is, whenever they start developing their plans on what they're going to do or sell or what service they're going to provide in order to make their money — they focus on ideas that are centered around what people need. But Robert J. Ringer, one of our favorite authors, has a saying: "If you have a business that sells people things they need, you might be able to make a nice living; but if you have a business that sells people something that they *want*, you can get rich." That's because people are selfish and self-motivated. We all are. We really want what we want, while we often turn our backs on what we need. Some of the basic needs, of course, we have to have: food, shelter, and that type of thing. Otherwise, most people are motivated by what they want, not by what's necessarily good for them or by what they really need.

Now, let's talk about something that people *do* really need in order to get rich. That's **Secret Number Thirteen** on our list: building a success library. This is something people desperately need in order to get rich, even though they often don't think that's the case. I know for a fact that some of you reading this publication are itching to know the mechanics of making money: you're thinking, "Come on. Tell me how to use the telephone answering machine or the voice mailbox. Come on, each me about classified advertising; teach me about direct mail. Teach me some of the direct-response techniques that I want to use." Well, this secret is an important one. We're laying a foundation here. It's kind of like making a cake; it's great to have the eggs, the shortening, the flour, and the sugar together, but if you don't have a plan, well, having them won't help you build a cake, especially if you don't know how much of each to use, how to mix them, and how to bake them together at the right temperature. Unless you already have some experience, you're not going to end up with a good cake just by guessing; you can go wrong without a plan.

Your foundation is simply this: you've got to be rich in your mind before you can be rich in your wallet. You have to learn before you can earn. In addition to advertising techniques, you have to know everything about what motivates the customer to buy. By learning this foundation, you're going to have a better chance to succeed. You need to expand your mind. Personally, I constantly read; I have thousands of books on many different subjects. With all the learning available today, a person just *has* to read more. That's why some people are so unsuccessful, I believe; they watch too much TV and they don't read. The person who *doesn't* read isn't any better off than the person who *can't* read. Reading books and business publications, and listening to audio recordings, is so essential to success. Eileen and I look at it as an investment, the best investment you can make — because once you expand your mind to new dimensions, it never goes back to its original shape.

Every time we go to the bookstore, we end up spending at least $200 on books. Our whole basement is covered with bookshelves and I think we have twelve or fourteen bookcases in the house. I'm not trying to make it sound like we're any better than anybody else, but we realized a long time ago that there are so many people who have shared all of their wisdom, their knowledge, and their ideas in the printed format, as a way of giving to and helping other people. All of that knowledge is available there, so we can read it and comprehend it and then use it. That's what we're trying to do with the Direct-Response Network.

You need to home in on specific kinds of books, too, covering the specific things that you want to learn about, for example, running your own business. There are thousands of books you can buy on that specific subject alone. There's just so much good information out there and I know that that has a lot to do with how much money that we, and our friends in this business, have made. I have to emphasize that I feel this is an important part of getting rich. Now, I can't stress it strongly enough that you don't have to fill your whole house and garage with books. If you're interested in marketing, you just read all the good marketing books. You should read books that help you set up a business and tell you what to do step-by-step. You should constantly be acquiring knowledge because that knowledge will translate into profits. Turn off that "boob tube" once in a while. Get a good book that can help you succeed and you'll enrich your life.

Secret Number Fourteen is to tap into the power of duplication. This is so powerful and so *necessary*. I mentioned this earlier, but I want to go over it again because of its importance. What you have to do, in my opinion, is discover how to make a little money. If someone can show me how they made $100 with a message on a computer bulletin board, on the Internet, with a small ad, or with a direct mailing, I can usually show that person how to make thousands or even millions of dollars using the power of duplication. First, find something that works! That's the key. It doesn't matter if it only makes you $50 or $100 at first. You can increase and duplicate that success by putting it into other publications and other media and really get something rolling that will bring in big-time money. Find something that makes a small profit, then keep adding the zeros. Get something that's working and then ask yourself how many different ways you can duplicate it — then, simply roll out with your profits. The only time it won't work — and this is very rare — is when you find a way to make a little money, but the marketplace is too small. If you're trying to sell to one-legged people in Cleveland, maybe you can't find enough of them. But if you have a big enough market, you can duplicate the zeros and you can roll out and make a lot of money.

In the last chapter, I talked about leverage. It seems that all rich people find as many ways as possible to use leverage and I feel I need to discuss that again. Everybody sees people with money and they think these folks are special or have some special talents or abilities. But many times, they're just thinking bigger and using as much leverage as they can. Leverage is the key to success in a situation like this. It relates to what I'm talking about with this secret: duplicating yourself, duplicating your messages, duplicating your ads. That's the power of direct-response marketing. Find something that works in a newspaper and then realize that there are 3,500 newspapers in America. It can happen even on a local basis: consider the jewelry store owner who gets one store working and then opens two, three, and four stores in the same city. Maybe, in addition to opening branch stores, he puts out a catalog so he can go beyond the bounds of the city and the neighborhood. Or, it's looking for distributors for your products or finding ways of hiring more people so that you can focus your time on a more conceptual overhead. When you learn how to make money, you can duplicate it.

One thing I wanted to add here is this: too many people think that having employees is a drain on your wallet. The fact is, my company wouldn't be here if we didn't have employees that we trusted to run the business while we were doing other things. It's nice to be able to go on vacation. It's nice to be able to truly be your own boss. So many times people get into businesses for themselves and they don't use leverage; they try to do everything themselves. They can only make so much money because they're not using any of these leverage principles that we're talking about and then they get totally burned out.

One great leverage principle in financial circles is using other people's money. In business, it's also a very powerful leverage tool to use other people's time, talent, and effort. Let me qualify this by saying that I realize that a lot of people are starting home businesses and, right at the beginning, it might be just a one-person business, or it might be a couple. In a situation like that, they can't really hire employees. That's okay; many of us started on our own. Once you become more successful, you can either hire employees or, if you love the home business and really don't want an outside office, you can hire independent contractors. You go to the typesetter; you go to the printer; you go to a copywriter. You go to all the different people who can enhance your business, but they don't have to be employees.

We didn't hire our first employee for 6-9 months after we knew the business was going to take off. It was so big by then that we just couldn't handle it ourselves. Even for the person who says, "Hey, I just don't want employees," then the independent contractor will also fill that void. Plus, there are temporary services in every town, if you just need somebody for a few hours a week — I think they require four hours minimum. The point is, you don't have to hire people in order to use these things. The subcontractors can come in many different shapes and forms. They pay the taxes and everything. You don't need to pay; you're just using the leverage that we talked about. I remember that when Al Galasso, the great direct-response marketer, was in California, he wouldn't hire employees on a regular basis; but he did run little ads in the *San Diego State Daily Aztec* whenever he wanted to get out big mailings or needed someone to do a lot of typesetting. Bingo! He'd have a few students over at his condo doing the work for him at a very reasonable price. There are always ways to get help.

Secret Number Fifteen is a subject that I think all of us could improve on: you must feel good about money. Now, I know a lot of people have negative programming when it comes to money, so it's vital to find out where your negative views, feelings, or attitudes are on the subject. Once you've discovered that, you have to find ways to correct those. Money is *not* the root of all evil, which even the Bible doesn't say if you read it closely. The Bible talks about the *love* of money being the root of all evil. In other words, if we love money more than we love people, we're in trouble.

We attract to ourselves that which we desire. There's nothing wrong with money. In fact, it's absolutely essential in our society. We should do everything possible to attract money rather than to repel it. Whenever I see a person who talks negatively about people with money, who is jealous, who is envious about wealthy people, I know that there's a person who's repelling money. Money won't come to the person who talks bad about it, who's always putting it down and is envious of other people that have it. Correct thinking about money is absolutely essential if you want to make a lot of it.

There's a mental law at work here: we will only attract to us that which we want. That which we're negative about or feel ill-at-ease about has a way of keeping away from us. Another thing: I believe that whatever you think about expands. It's simple. You tell people that they have to start thinking about money more in order to get any money and the first thing they say to you is, "What do you mean? Money is all I think about!" But when you actually start talking to them, you find that all of their conversations about money and all of the thinking that they do about money isn't things like, "How are we going to get more money? How can we make more money? What services can we provide to earn more money?" No, all of the thinking they do about money is more along the lines of, "How are we going to pay all of our bills this month? How are we ever going to get that bill taken care of? How can we afford this?" It always has to do with the limitations of budgeting money and that's negative, I think.

Russ von Hoelscher told me about a seminar in Minneapolis-St. Paul a few year back where he had a black entrepreneur come up to him — a man who was really going places with his own books, tapes, and other materials related to success. He told Russ that one of the problems in minority communities is that, too often, the leaders in those communities tell the people what they have to get from the government. He said, "This is wrong." This is a black man speaking from a position of power and I think he knew what he was talking about. He said that once he realized that he was as good as anyone else, there was no reason he couldn't enjoy the American dream. So he took the bull by the horns. He started a business in his spare time and he said success came to him quickly. He said a lot of people (and this is true of whites, blacks, Hispanics, and others) are taught by parents, teachers, and leaders that money is scarce. There are the haves and there are the have-nots. Well, if you buy into that mentality, it will keep you in poverty. It was so powerful, what this man had to say before the group. He said that once he realized that he could have the American dream, and he wasn't going to listen to the leaders who were always were talking about how we have to get increases in welfare and we have to get more from the government, he decided, "No, within me are the seeds of power and the seeds of wealth." He just took off tremendously.

Let's talk about all of the people who, all of their lives, have been exposed to "job" kind of thinking. They're always thinking, "How am I going to get that job? How am I going to keep that job once I have it?" They don't think enough of prosperity, in the sense of, "How can I start my own enterprise? What can I do to serve other people? What kind of products can I sell? What kind of services can I market?" All of their thinking is oriented around a job — and as I mentioned in an earlier chapter, you're never going to get rich working for someone else. I once watched a C-SPAN program called *Germany Revisited* and it told about how East and West Germany were now reunited. The mentality of some of the East Germans was telling: they lived under Communism for about fifty years. They worked in factories or they worked in offices. They always worked for the state. They were told what to do and when to do it. They had very little control over their lives.

So they were interviewing some entrepreneurs in East Germany. One started a restaurant; others started other types of businesses. One was saying that one of the hardest things to learn was that he was now responsible for his own life and that he could go as far as he wanted. He had to use the marketing principles and he had to use good business principles. He was telling how hard it was because, when you live under a Communist regime, you do what you're told when you're told. You don't think for yourself. Well, thank heaven we don't live under such a regime in America — but still, it's amazing how many of us are almost like robots. We just go and do the same thing day after day after day. Well, as the old cliché says, "If you always do what you've always done, you'll always get what you've always gotten." We have to break free from that type of robotic living and take some initiative if we're going to start and succeed in business. A lot of people leave their mommies and daddies, who took care of them, and go to the government instead — or to an employer. When you're on a job you also have people telling you what to do all the time, so, you never have to think for yourself.

This is a powerful principle and you should highlight it in this publication right here and now. *Start thinking for yourself.* Don't just listen to other people. Above all, at least don't listen to other people without questioning them. Even more importantly, please, please, *please*, don't give in to this negative thinking which often comes from people around us. It absolutely will destroy your success.

CHAPTER 4:

Secrets Sixteen Through Twenty

Our **Secret Number Sixteen** is just this: the importance of knowing yourself. All of us have certain strengths and certain weaknesses. Knowing them is real power. Eileen and I didn't start making a lot of money until we realized that she's good at doing certain things and I'm good at doing other things. It's this synergy between our talents that has created our own wealth. It's important to develop your own inner power, to know exactly what you're best at, and then to put your energy into all those things you're best at.

Another thing I want to say about knowing yourself is that you must understand human nature and, of course, that comes from knowing yourself. Think about the things you desire. Think about the things you fear. Think about what your concerns are. Then, you can take that information that comes from within and realize that there are millions of other people just like you. See, that's the great secret that's really not a secret. Most people are pretty much alike. There are different ethnic groups and there are certainly people who come from different financial situations — but at the core, we're all pretty much the same. When you know more about yourself, then you can start making offers and you can put together products and touch people, just by knowing what you want and desire and the things you're fearful of, then you translate those into offers for other people.

More specifically than that, you should intimately know

your market. When Eileen and I got into the business, we already knew the opportunity market — the market we've made our millions in — because we were such good customers for so many years and because we were buying all of these get-rich-quick books ourselves, along with all kinds of money-making plans and business opportunities. Because we were spending so much of our money buying all of those things, when we decided to get into the market and we developed our own money-making plan, the Dialing-For-Dollars program, we already knew what those millions of people wanted.

That's a major key to success in any business: understanding your market completely. You do that by reading about the market, by getting on all the mailing lists, by buying products from competitors or potential competitors, and absolutely understanding everything you can about that market. When we know something like the palm of your hand, we can take the actions that will bring tremendous profit.

Secret Number Seventeen is pyramiding your profits. Everybody's heard of cash flow; even people who don't understand much about business use that word quite liberally. What exactly is a cash flow? We look at it as a river that runs right through our company. As long as we keep that river flowing by putting more of our profits back into what made us the profits to begin with, we can keep the cash flowing. What you have to do is continue to continue. By that, I mean that once they get an offer that's working, you have to continue using it. In direct-response marketing, it doesn't make any sense to quit marketing, for example, in the summertime. It used to be an old wives' tale that you couldn't sell in the summer. Yes, sales may go down a little bit in the summer compared to the fall and winter, but you still have to keep the river running; you have to have the cash flow coming in. So, continue to market. Make a plan so that you do something every single week that helps increase your business.

Most people want to make money so badly that once they *do* start making money, they don't put any money back into the business to make more money. That's the whole thing about the power of pyramiding your profits. You can take the profits from two ads and then leverage that into two more; now you have four ads. Then, you take the profits from those four ads and leverage them into eight ads. Pretty soon, you can have hundreds of ads out there, given the power of duplication. Whatever you put it back into, pretty soon you can have lots of different things making you money. The person who takes the money that they make originally and goes out and buys a new car, well, that's nice, but the smart entrepreneur knows that a large part of every dollar that comes in should be put back into the business so you can build this leverage. So you can go from two ads to four, four to eight, and eight to sixteen. Eventually, you'll have a river of profit — and you can get the home, the car, the boat, and everything else that goes with it.

We once had a distributor whose sole purpose in having the distributorship was to pay off his house loan. Once he paid off his house loan, he was done; he didn't want a business. However, two or three years later he came back and said, "Hey, I want to start to make some more money again!" It just shows that everybody has different needs. If all you want to do is pay off a loan or help put the kids through college, once the kid is out of college you can say, "Okay, that's it. I'm not going to do this anymore." Well, God bless you — but boy-oh-boy, why not build a tremendous business that's perpetual, that just goes on and on? In the long run, it will be so satisfying and so rewarding. If our distributor had taken out money that he paid off his house with and duplicated it by buying more ads and that kind of thing, he would have had more money to pay off his house, buy a new car, put the kids through school, and then retire with.

Eileen and I have a saying that goes like this: the solution to all of our business problems is simply to make more money. Earlier, I talked about how you should feel good about money and I talked about prosperity. You should always look for ways to make more money. Success is the journey; the success is the business and we should love our business because we are very much involved in it. We look forward to it. I've noticed that almost all of the successful people I've met people over the past 25 years really enjoying what they're doing. I've talked about this previously, but it bears repeating. When you love what you're doing, you never work hard, even if you work long hours. It's an exciting and rich way to live. Though, admittedly, sometimes it tends to be a little bit lonely because you're out there all by yourself. Being an entrepreneur is to be a minority. Most people have jobs and most people just want to put in their 40 hours and then get off work and that's it.

Let's move on to **Secret Number Eighteen**, which is: if you want to get rich, you have to have some type of support. If you can get it from your boyfriend, girlfriend, or spouse, that's wonderful. Here's what I say. If you can't get your support at home, if family isn't going to give you that support — and sometimes they don't — then you should search for a business friend, a kindred spirit, someone in your own area preferably, that you can partner up with. Even if it's a long-distance friendship via telephone, find someone else in business that you can communicate with. You can support him or her and he or she can support you. Then, of course, I also believe you need a mentor. I know that, for myself, having Eileen involved in the business and us doing this together as a team, with her running the business and me doing the marketing, we have that bond. We talk to a lot of people about that: about the power of a couple working together. Some people think that that can't work, but I really believe that it can. I know that all I can speak for is our success, but having the two of us working together in this synergistic effort has just been such a powerful force for us.

If a person doesn't have that ideal relationship, they still need a support system. The network, we're putting together will also serve as a support system. We'll be in touch with our members and it's a good way for them to have an overview of what we can teach, though they should also seek in their own area someone who believes the way they believe — someone who believes in their dreams, someone who will really support them while they, in turn, support the other person. It makes all the difference in the world to have someone who believes in you. There are even those who say that if you *don't* have support of people around you, you should get rid of them. That's pretty harsh! Of course, "getting rid of them" could just mean cutting off your hearing so you don't hear the negative stuff that they say. In other words, you can't buy into their negativity, even though you still love them or respect them. Their negativity may be due to some of their own problems. Earlier, I talked about the limitations that people have, or the ideas they have, about money being limited. I think that's where some of this general negativity comes from. Whatever the case, you need a support system. To have a friend, you have to be a friend, so find someone who will support you so, in return, you support them.

Secret Number Nineteen is to focus on serving others. Since day one, Eileen and I have listened to the advice of the great motivational speaker Zig Ziegler. We've heard him talk in person and we've bought some of his books. He had this one saying that stuck with us, so we made it one of our foundational beliefs: "You can have whatever you want in life, if you simply help enough other people get what *they* want." As a matter of fact, we believed in that so much that the very first book we ever published had that right on the back cover. I know that's a belief that has helped us make a lot of money and I really do think it's one of the greatest internal success principles.

There seems to be some type of a spiritual plus, a financial law that rewards people who help others. Hopefully, you're doing it because you want to do it and you really care about other people, but even if you don't care about other people, if you help them anyhow, you seem to be richly rewarded for it. Help enough people to get what they want and these people will then help you get what you want.

A practical example of that is the way Eileen and I work with suppliers. We work with a couple of printers who have built huge businesses by finding out all the things that their customers, or their prospects, hate in other printers. For example, other printers are very slow in getting bids and delivering jobs. Any time a person simply finds a way of solving problems that people have with other businesses, they can get very rich. It's a way of serving people. Another thing that we often do is that when we make an offer to someone, we try to make a complete offer. We try to give that person all the components they need to get started, rather than doing things in a helter-skelter partial sort of way. I think that that's very important because your customer gets something with very little assembly required; people really appreciate this.

The stronger the offer, the stronger the promise you're making to the customer. That's service; that's giving people what they want. The companies that are out there making millions of dollars have simply found a way to give their customers the things they want better than any other company does. As I mentioned earlier, people feel isolated. *All* people feel isolated. They hunger for attention and support, which is why I believe it's a great idea to put a phone number in your literature. Even if you can't answer all the calls when people make them, it means so much to the person that you really care and you're willing to share. Make some callbacks. Don't be afraid to talk to your customers. Some people in mail order say, "Gee, I don't want any dealings with the customer. That's why I'm only going to take orders by mail." Well, you have to rethink that premise because people like to communicate in more ways than just by mail. You can make a lot of money by communicating with your customers and showing them that you really do care.

Here's **Secret Number Twenty**. If you can just learn how to do this more, you can increase your chances of success by 1000%. I'm convinced of that. Here it is: take risks. The people who are out there that are getting rich, the ones making the most money possible, are people who know how to take risks. I realize that being in business is scary sometimes; trying new things is frightening for a lot of people. In fact, I think fear and the fear of taking risks stops 80% of potential entrepreneurs from going forward. It's natural to feel uncomfortable trying something new, which is why you need to make a small start. Continue with your present job if you're working for someone else, but make a small start and learn as you earn. Take baby steps before you try to take your bigger, giant steps. You'll encounter small successes and your confidence will go up. It's like putting a few toes in the water; once you're used to the temperature, you can put your feet in. Pretty soon, you're not as afraid of the water and you start to go out a little bit deeper. Start small, if you have this fear, but *START*.

The one thing that prevents success more than anything else is simply the failure to start. My wife Eileen likes to tell people, "Just get started. Even if you make mistakes, go ahead and just do it." There's a lot of power in getting any kind of a start. You know, people have these false ideas about entrepreneurs. They see us taking all kinds of risks and assume we're fearless. Well, I happen to know that Eileen and I are scared of taking risks, too. But we've learned that the only way that you can ever really profit is by sticking your neck out. Be willing to take risks. The more you do it, the more confidence you get, and the better you get at all of this.

So if you see entrepreneurs out there whose every touch just seems to turn to gold, don't think, "My God, what is it about these people? They're blessed. They have some special talents." It's not true. The only thing that entrepreneurs have that you don't is more experience.

CHAPTER 5:

The Last Five Secrets

Okay, folks, we're entering the home stretch! We're up to **Secret Number Twenty-One,** which is vital to any entrepreneur: you have to learn discipline. Once you start your business, you have to learn discipline to keep on keeping on; you're not going to be able to continue through sheer momentum. You have to make some little sacrifices to accomplish this — for example, you have to watch less television. I know I harp on that a lot, but I do think TV is a big success robber. You also have to start from the beginning as you build your business. Maybe nobody's looking over your shoulder, making you do it — but we're in business for ourselves, so we have to supervise ourselves. If you slough off, you're hurting yourself directly.

Secret Number Twenty-Two is the power of action. Simply put, there's nothing that can replace action. The best ideas in the world won't make you a dime until you do something with them. You have to figure out a plan, list all the actions you can take, and then you simply have to get started. Find out what works best for you and correct it as you go along. This relates to what I just talked about in the last two secrets. Make a start. Be persistent. Do something every day. Keep moving forward! There's such power in forward motion. There's a Chinese saying: "A thousand-mile journey begins with but a single step." I've found that when I'm working on a major project, the minute I start, I feel like the job is half done. So much time and effort is wasted in thinking about how to start, when to start, and whether you should start. Just *getting started* puts you well down the road.

You figure things out as you go. Lots of times, people are confused until they get started — but as they commit to something, they start figuring things out, and **Secret Number Twenty-Three** is: they start developing a body of specialized knowledge. This is something that Napoleon Hill talks about lot about in *Think and Grow Rich* as one of his fundamental success principles. As you get started, you develop specialized knowledge; you should make it your avocation to be as learned as possible in certain areas. General knowledge is great, but to really make money you need to specialize. In other words, zero in on a certain segment of the market you're doing business with. Do things that will teach you everything we need to know about a certain discipline, a certain type of information, a certain type of very specialized information that people want. When you do that, we can make a lot of money with it. Too many people are trying to be something for everyone. The real power lies in focusing on a specific area and then doing that better than anybody else can. I've seen many people become millionaires just by carving out a small niche in the market. In fact, it's called niche marketing. When you become the best you can be, and offer the best service and products to a niche market, you'll be rewarded beyond belief.

Too many people are too scattered in their business approaches. They have too many things going through their minds at any one time. They want to try everything under the sun. Another thing: don't try to start about five, six, or seven different businesses at a time. I talked to a guy once who was starting with about three multi-level companies, plus he wanted to sell books by mail — plus, he'd had some gadgets that he was going to get from Taiwan and sell. I told him "This is too many things. It's better to do one or two things good than to just scatter yourself all over the map." Stay focused!

Secret Number Twenty-Four is: you have to think about making money every single day. I say that simply because the more you think about it, the more you start developing your ideas. Oftentimes people want to make money, but they forget that you don't just start out on Day One having it all figured out. Sometimes your ideas have to develop as you go; they have to grow and expand. By thinking about making money all the time, you start maturing your whole thinking process. You start getting better ideas. One of the best ways to get better ideas is to get up in the morning and spend some time with a pen and a yellow tablet. Try to do it at least three or four times a week, whether it be for twenty minutes, a half hour, an hour, or more. Write down all the things you can do that would be profitable for you, both in the financial and personal senses.

The rewards from spending that time with yourself are immense because it really adds up. When you think about it, that's over 300 hours every year that you're spending focused and concentrated. Here's what's going to happen — I speak from experience here. A lot of the ideas that I had twenty years ago, at the beginning of my marketing career, were just the stupidest ideas ever. Now that I look back, I thank God that I never tried to put some of those ideas into action. They just weren't very good ideas. But the longer you do this, the more you develop your thinking process, the more you start finding all of the things that really do work, and the more you start being able to think things through the right way. That's when your ideas really get power. Even the seed inside a bad idea can develop into a new, good idea; that is, even ideas that don't pan out often turn in a different direction and lead to great new successes. I just believe in ideas, period. Eventually, great ideas will emerge if you just continue to exercise your brain.

One of the purposes of the Direct-Response Network is to give all of our members powerful ideas that can really make a difference in their lives. That's **BONUS SECRET Number Twenty-Five**: get involved in the Direct-Response Network. The purpose of the network is to help average people make above-average incomes. I'm here to tell you that it's possible for anybody who wants to make money to do so. I don't care if you're on welfare; I don't care how much in debt you are. Sometimes, in fact, being in debt can be one of your biggest motivators. Anybody in this country who has a desire to get rich and make a lot of money can do it. The purpose of the Direct-Response Network is to help all of our members, to give them the ideas, to give them the encouragement, the motivation, and the tools necessary to be able to reach those goals for themselves. This is something that's going to benefit thousands of people because it can help you leapfrog your way to success. As I close this publication, I'm going to go over several ways that the Direct-Response Network can help you, based on the 24 Secrets to Getting Rich that I've just covered.

First of all, we can help give you the support you need. That was Secret Number Eighteen. We can help you learn how to take risks by encouraging you. That was Secret Number Twenty. Month after month, you're going to get powerful money-making ideas. The more you hear all of this, the more it helps to make things easier for you. Secret Number Twenty-Four, which we just talked about, is thinking about making money every single day. You can bet we'll help with that! Part of the reason we've put these consulting packages together is so that we can give you new ideas constantly. Getting this material every month will help keep you focused, will help you develop your thinking process about making money. We'll also help you feel good about money: that was Secret Number Fifteen.

Every single month, as we share new ideas, new methods, and strategies, we'll encourage you on all those points. We're going to be talking a lot about selling people what they want, *not* what they need, and about all the different principles I've discussed here. Every single month we're going to find new ways to expand on all of this. We'll get teach you exactly how to write a classified ad, how to do display ads, how to use voice mailbox systems, and how to use television advertising at the lowest possible cost. We're going to show you every single way to market your products and services and show you the best way to market them in every single area.

There are millions of people who need to learn how to make money. This is one thing that really bothers Eileen and I: we see all these people out there struggling. Let's face it, to be in the job market these days is to be pretty insecure. There used to be a time when you were able to go to work for a major corporation, put in thirty or thirty-five years, and end up with a gold watch and a good retirement plan. You just can't do that anymore. Times are changing. The time to become an entrepreneur and start making money on your own is *right now*.

We're very excited about the future because we realize that more and more, as technology advances, as personal computers develop, and as services like fax machines and Federal Express become common, financial freedom is becoming more and more of a reality. You can live any where in the world you want to live and have all these tools and resources you need to develop and sustain your business. Average people like Eileen and I, who live in the tiny town of Goessel, Kansas, can succeed and make it big. If you look at a map, you can't even find Goessel, Kansas; — we're out in the middle of nowhere!

We're living proof that you can use technology to succeed, no matter where you are in the work. With all the current technological developments, and all the wonderful things coming up in the next few years, it's the perfect time to strike out on your own and learn to use the Secrets to Getting Rich to make your own fortune. So get on out there and *just do it!*